ANIMAL TRUNK

SILLY POEMS

TO READ ALOUD

Charles Ghigna

ILLUSTRATED BY **Gabriel**

HARRY N. ABRAMS, INC., PUBLISHERS

Chickens peck.
Chickens peep.
Chickens cluck
In their sleep.

Chickens roost.
Chickens lay
Chicken eggs
Everyday.

Chickens live
In a coop.
Chickens hate
Chicken soup.

CHICKENS

Bears are playful.
Bears are round.
Grizzly bears
Are dressed in brown.

Bears like honey.
Bears like trees.
Bears are chased
By honeybees.

Bears like mountains.
Bears like streams.
Bears spend winters
In their dreams.

BEARS

Donkeys heehaw.
Donkeys bray.
Donkeys kick
And donkeys play.

Donkeys run.
Donkeys dart.
Donkeys pull
A donkey cart.

Brother to
The horse and mule,
Donkeys think
That donkeys rule!

DONKEYS

Cows like sunshine.
Cows like mud.
Cows like chewing
On their cud.

Cows like hillsides.
Cows like trails.
Cows like waving
Swishy tails.

Cows like mooing.
Cows like hay.
Cows like giving
Milk each day.

COWS

Giraffes

It's easy to laugh
At the tall giraffe
Each time we go to the zoo.

But it can't be much fun
With his head in the sun.
Giraffes may need sunglasses too!

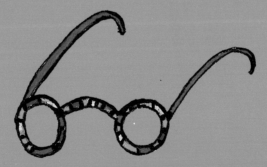

Bunnies nibble.
Bunnies doze.
Bunnies twitch
A bunny nose.

Bunnies huddle.
Bunnies hide.
Bunnies like to
Dig outside.

Bunnies run.
Bunnies stop.
Bunnies do
The bunny hop.

BUNNIES

Like jungle men
From outer space,
Monkeys wear
A funny face.

Monkeys like to
Taunt and tease.
Monkeys do
As monkeys please.

Monkeys like to
Laugh and play
Monkey business
Every day.

MONKEYS

There's nothing like
A bunch of puppies,
Not even bowls
Of baby guppies.

When you run
They like to chase.
When you stop
They lick your face.

When they chew
The morning mail,
Puppies wag
A happy tail.

PUPPIES

Goats like kicking
Up their heels.
Goats like eating
Junkyard meals.

Goats like showing off
Their grins
Just above their
Bearded chins.

Goats like playing
In the sun.
Goats like butting
Just for fun!

GOATS

CROCODILES

Crocodiles sun.
Crocodiles nap.
Crocodiles yawn.
Crocodiles snap.

Crocodiles crawl.
Crocodiles charge.
Crocodiles´ teeth
Are very, very large.

Crocodiles run.
Crocodiles pause.
Crocodiles crunch
Their giant jaws!

Curled up in
A ball of fur,
Kittens mew,
Kittens purr.

Kittens like to
Climb and see
All the birds
Up in the tree.

Kittens tumble.
Kittens play,
Inside outside
Every day.

KITTENS

Lambs are woolly.
Lambs are warm.
Lambs are chilly
When they're shorn.

Lambs are cozy.
Lambs are cute.
Lambs give you
Your winter suit.

When they grow up
Lambs are sheep.
Counting them
Puts you to sleep.

LAMBS

Tigers prowl.
Tigers pace.
Tigers wear
A scary face.

With stripes upon
Their coats of fur,
Tigers prance,
Tigers purr.

Tigers leap.
Tigers play.
Tigers always
Get their way.

TIGERS

SNAKES

Snakes are slender.
Snakes are sleek.
Snakes like playing
Hide-and-seek.

Snakes are sneaky.
Snakes are sly.
Snakes will look you
In the eye.

Snakes are clever.
Snakes are fast.
If you see one
Let it pass.